INSTANT GOLF LESSONS

£4.50

INSTANT GOLF LESSONS

By the Editors of Golf Digest
Illustrations by Elmer Wexler and Stan Drake

A Golf Digest Book

Published by
Golf Digest
A New York Times Company
495 Westport Avenue
Norwalk, Connecticut 06856

Trade book distribution
by Simon and Schuster
A Division of Gulf & Western Corporation
New York, New York 10020

First Printing
ISBN: 0-914178-16-4
Library of Congress: 77-92907
Manufactured in the United States of America

INTRODUCTION

Instant Golf Lessons is a compilation of 112 of the finest instant lessons that have appeared in *Golf Digest* magazine through the years. It has been designed for easy, visual instruction that will stay with you on the golf course during your most critical shots.

Taken from the first-hand teaching experiences of some of the leading club professionals and touring pros around the country, each lesson is quick to read, easy to understand and contains one, key element to help your game. And each one is illustrated with a simple drawing by Stan Drake or Red Wexler to convey the point visually. To ensure that they are based on sound principles and solid techniques, the lessons have been reviewed and approved by the Golf Digest Professional Teaching Panel, which has included the most distinguished teachers of the game: Bob Toski, Jim Flick, Eddie Merrins, Henry Ransom and Paul Runyan.

Instant Golf Lessons is arranged by parts of the swing or game—grip, set-up, backswing, slicing, pitching, etc.

To use the book most effectively, you can read it through and absorb the lessons one by one—or you can keep it handy for those times when a particular area needs work. If you develop a problem, you will almost certainly be able to pinpoint a cure by referring to that section. And, as an added bonus, a special chapter on practice drills is designed to help you groove your swing before you reach the first tee.

Instant Golf Lessons was compiled to cure your swing faults. The overall results, we hope, will improve your confidence, your concentration and—eventually your scores.

—*The Editors*

CONTENTS

GRIP

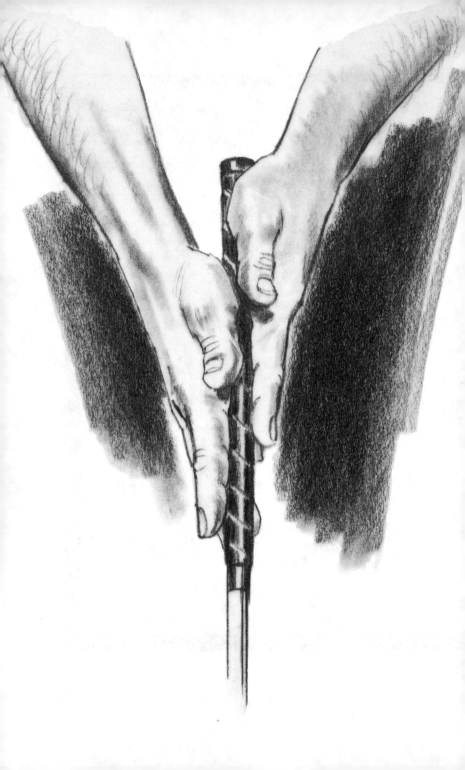

Grip with palms facing for accurate shots

Your grip controls to a great degree the direction your clubface will be looking at impact. The best way to assure that the clubface will be looking at the target is to grip with your hands more or less facing each other.

To accomplish this, place the club shaft between your hands, the palms facing one another. Slide the right hand down enough so that you can take a comfortable grip, keeping the palms facing one another and aligned with a square clubface.

Beginners may need to use a stronger grip—the hands turned more to the right on the shaft. This tends to create more hand action and compensates for the novice's tendency to slice. But even when assuming a stronger grip, the palms should be kept more or less parallel to assure consistent results.

—Harold Blaylock

11

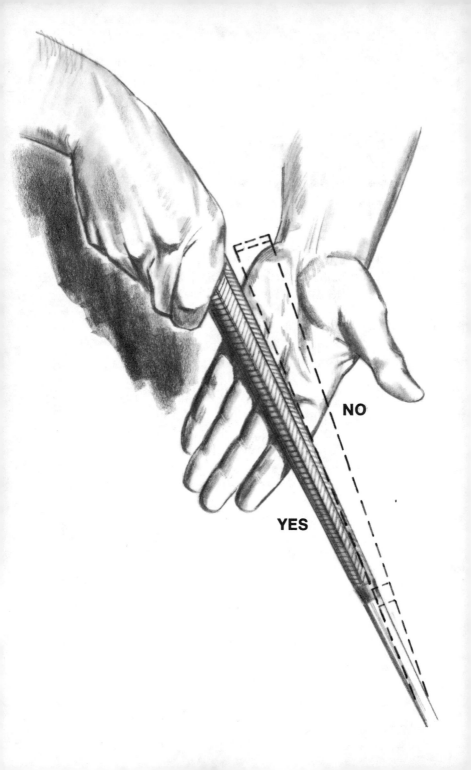

Grip under pad for more control

An incorrect left-hand grip results in a sloppy hold on the club at the top of the backswing, which in turn causes misdirected shots. When you let go with the left hand at the top, you must re-grip on the way down. At this point the right hand usually takes over, altering clubface alignment and clubhead path and causing inaccuracy.

A correct left-hand grip has the club running diagonally just above the roots of the fingers and resting just below the heel pad of the hand. When you fold your hand over the club, it should anchor snugly below the pad. When the club rests too high on the heel pad (see incorrect drawing), your control is reduced. —*The Editors*

13

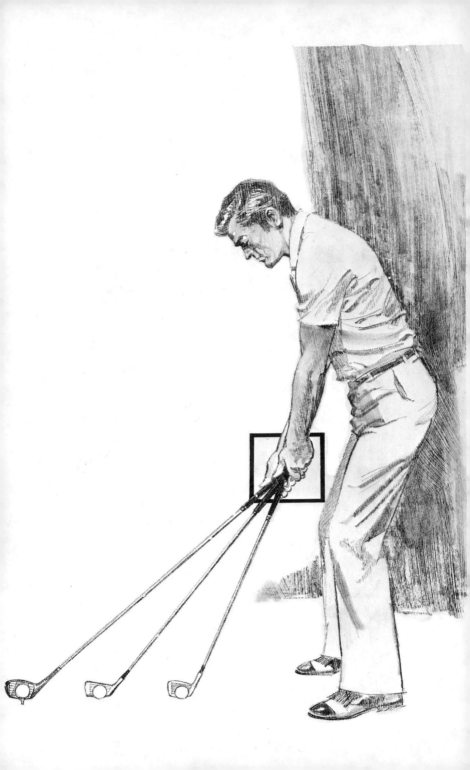

Start each swing from same hand position

Proper hand position at address is a key to developing a repeating swing. At address on all full shots, you should position your hands the same height from the ground, opposite the same portion of your body, and the same distance from your body. The only variable required by a change of clubs is in the distance of the ball from your body. The distance should gradually increase with the longer clubs.

During play you should occasionally check the placement of your hands as you take your address position. For consistency, make sure that you are "dropping" your hands into the same relative position every time.

—*Babe Lichardus*

15

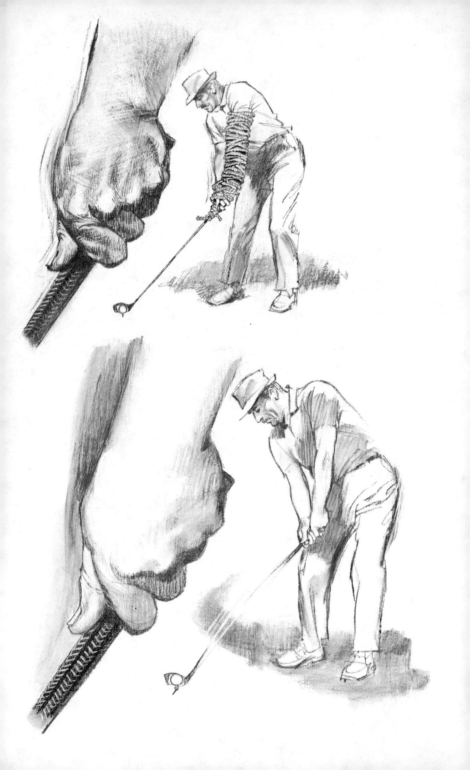

Ease grip pressure to increase club speed

Extreme grip pressure can severely restrict your golf swing, particularly your arm and shoulder movement.

If you are holding the club too tightly, a more relaxed, but still firm, grip can add yardage for two reasons. First, such a grip relaxes your shoulders and allows you to increase your upper-body coiling on your backswing. Second, the reduction of tension will help you release your hands and wrists more fluidly during impact.

—*Barney Corrigan*

17

Finish with firm grip for solid strokes

Firmness of grip on the club is essential to solid striking. If your hands loosen before or during impact, the clubhead will stutter and probably change alignment, reducing distance and accuracy.

I suggest you consciously make sure your hands are firm at the finish of each swing. If they are still firm there, you will have maintained that firmness through impact.   —*William Kittleman*

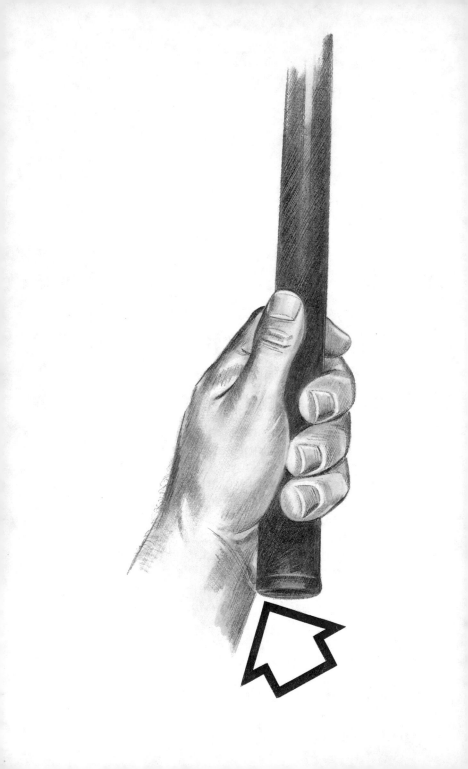

A checkpoint for grip length

Gripping the club too long can cause many swing ailments. If the butt end of the club presses into the heel pad of your left hand, you may lose control of the club at the top of your backswing. This can cause you to re-grip the club on your downswing and slow down your arm swing through the ball. By gripping the club so the butt end is even with the edge of the heel of your left hand, you will retain control throughout your swing. This will create confidence and lower scores.

—*Pat Reilly*

SETUP

1

2

3

Stand up and take a bow

You need proper posture at the ball before you can possibly make a good swing. By following these three steps, you will not only automatically achieve the correct address position, but also you will properly balance your weight between the heel and ball of each foot.

1. Stand up straight and erect, with feet shoulder width apart. Hold the club out in front (with the proper grip) so that the clubhead is about 18 inches off the ground and the grip end points at your left hip. Keep your left arm straight with your elbows close together.

2. Bend forward from the hips, with your back straight, until the clubhead reaches the ground. Don't make any other movement.

3. Flex your knees slightly.

—Jim Geram

Set up with right side low and lazy

Many golfers never give themselves a chance to make a good swing because, in setting up to the ball, the right side is in a dominant position.

The right hand clutches the club too powerfully which sets the right arm and shoulder higher than the left. This encourages the right-hander's natural tendency to lift the club with his right hand and arm during the backswing, which restricts his shoulder turn and throws the club outside the target line on the downswing.

Set up with your right side "underneath" (as though some outside force were employing a crowbar on you— see illustration). Your right hand, arm and side should be relaxed and submissive to your left side, which is firmly in control. Your left arm should be straight (not stiff) and slightly higher than the right at address.

—*Joe Cannon*

27

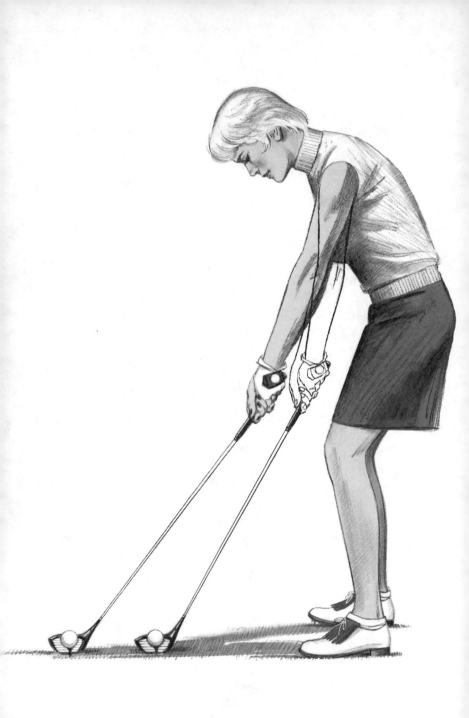

Ladies: reaching's a must to clear your bust

Women golfers have a problem unique to their sex. Their bust-lines often interfere with a free swing, particularly if their hands are too close to their bodies at address. To avoid this tendency take your proper grip on the club and extend your arms straight out at shoulder height. Flex your knees slightly and bend over from the hips until the club touches the ground. Now you'll be in the perfect address position, on the way to an unimpeded swing.　　　　—*Debbie Austin*

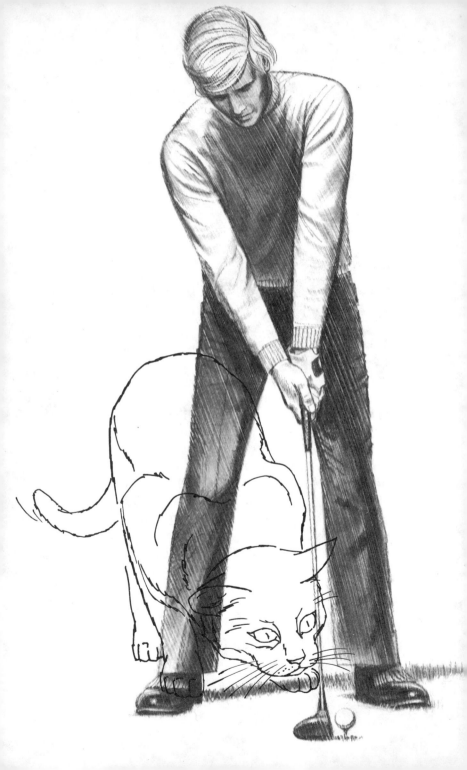

Cat-like stance promotes power

All good athletes assume a cat-like stance before they move into action. This is achieved by maintaining weight toward the forward part of their feet. This keeps the leg muscles loose but alive, in a state of readiness.

For golfers, this promotes participation of the legs in the swing, a vital factor in building power and distance. Those who start the swing with "dead" or motionless feet will swing almost solely with the arms and upper body and will severely limit their power.

During the forward press that precedes the backswing, press down on the balls of your feet. Your heels will not rise, of course, but you should feel less weight or pressure there. This will give you the lively legs that will add yards to your shots.   —*Sam Urzetta*

31

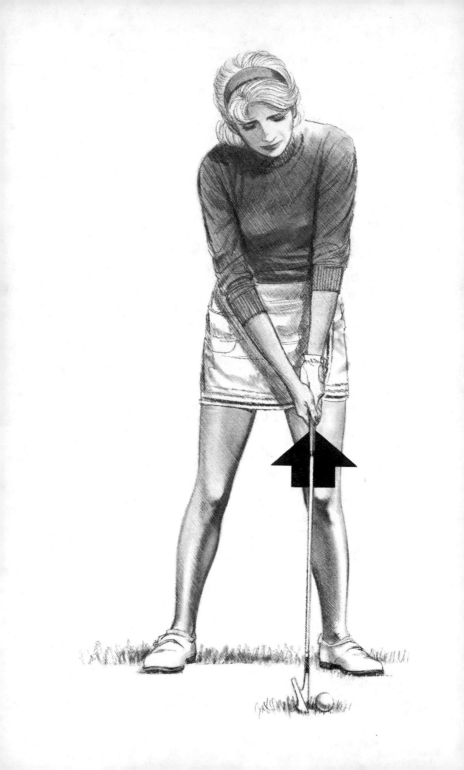

Left hand over left knee irons out problems

Three important components of the swing with the irons will automatically fall in place if a golfer follows this simple address precept: *See that your left hand is over your left knee.* This will:

1. Result in a straight arm-clubshaft line that if maintained will produce a strong backswing body-coil and a steady swing arc.

2. Position your hands correctly ahead of the clubhead and help you lead the downswing with your left side, which improves clubhead speed.

3. Help you swing so that the clubface pinches the ball against the turf for maximum backspin and accuracy.

—*Margie Masters*

Take a fighting stance

Imagine I'm going to punch you in the nose. What kind of stance would you take? You'd probably assume almost a squatting posture, solid on your feet with knees flexed, ready to move quickly.

That's also how you should set up to a golf shot. Many players stand too casually erect. Perhaps they fear that if they sit down to the ball at address they will raise up on their downswing. Just the opposite is true. With your knees flexed and your back straight, you'll stay down with the shot and, with more leg flexibility, drive your lower body toward the target. You'll gain in both power and accuracy.

The importance of good knee-flex became obvious to me early in my career because I'm unusually tall for a golfer. But, regardless of size, everyone should assume a fighting stance.

—*George Archer*

ALIGNMENT

Use a T-square to the target

Unless a golfer is properly aligned to the target, it is virtually impossible for him to develop a sound golf swing. Copying the formation of the carpenter's T-square will help you achieve this proper alignment.

At address, your right foot should form the vertical section of the square, with the line to the target being the horizontal or crossing section.

In assuming a stance, first place your right foot in the described position. Now move your left foot to the target side of the ball, turning the toe out but keeping the heel the same distance from the target line as the right heel. You then will be in perfect alignment. —*Roland Harper*

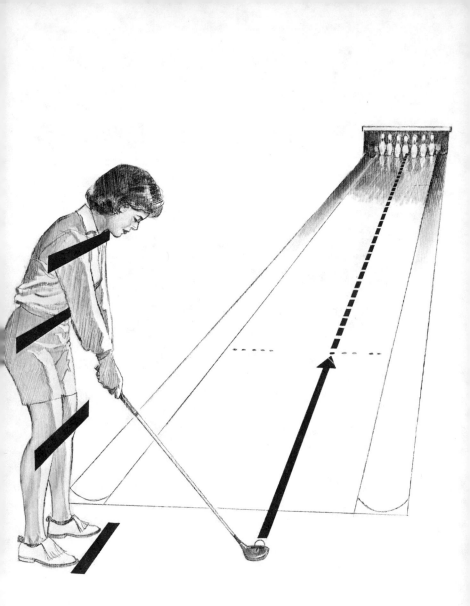

Pick a spot, then align your shot

It is natural for your golf shots to follow the alignment of your hips and shoulders. If they are properly aligned at address, you are more likely to hit the shot where you had intended.

To make certain I am aligned correctly, I go through a "spot check," borrowed from bowling, before every shot. From behind the ball, I select a spot on the ground some three feet ahead and on line to the target. I have in mind hitting the ball over that spot, much like a bowler would roll over a pre-selected spot on the lane. Keeping that spot in mind, I align my hips and shoulders parallel to the line.

You may find it easier to align with the spot than with the much more distant target. —*Donna Caponi Young*

Align body to clubface

A golfer should let the clubface—once the clubhead has been correctly positioned—determine his body alignment, rather than to let his body position determine clubface aim. By placing the clubhead on the ground behind the ball so that the face is looking down the intended line, the golfer achieves a constant reference point that will never lead him astray.

The proper procedure is to first position the clubhead as described. Then, with the right foot in position and holding the club with only the right hand, step back slightly with the left foot so that you are almost facing the target. Re-check your aim at this point, adjust the clubface alignment, if necessary, and then move into a final address position which you feel will best accommodate a swing along the chosen line. Don't move the club as you step into your stance.   —*Chick Harbert*

Check stance to assure it is square

A golfer can detect alignment flaws and improve his positioning with this practice method:

Place a club on the ground parallel to the intended line of flight so that the club lies between your feet and the ball (see illustration). Then take your stance so that the toe of each shoe is equidistant from the club. Also align your knees, hips and shoulders so that a line across each parallels the club.

This is the basic "square" stance, recommended for all golfers. Such a stance encourages a swing that will bring the clubhead into the ball exactly along the target line, thus producing maximum accuracy. After some practice with the "target" club on the ground, you will automatically take a properly aligned stance in actual play.

—*Howell Fraser*

BACKSWING

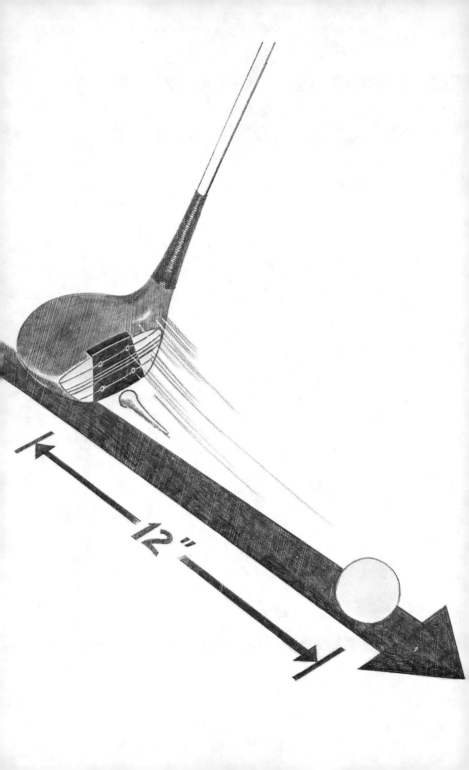

12"

Brush wood tee for low-slow takeaway

Here's how I make sure that my backswing starts "slow and low" and along the path that I want for accuracy and power. I lay a wooden tee on the grass, about 12 inches behind the ball and along my takeaway line which, at that point, is slightly inside that target line. Then, with my left arm straight, I push the clubhead back along the grass until it touches the tee. Only then do I let the clubhead rise. Using this technique, I go through a warm-up drill from middle irons to driver. Then, in actual play where such practice aids are forbidden, it's no trick at all to just imagine the same line and repeat the same kind of swing.   —*David Allaire*

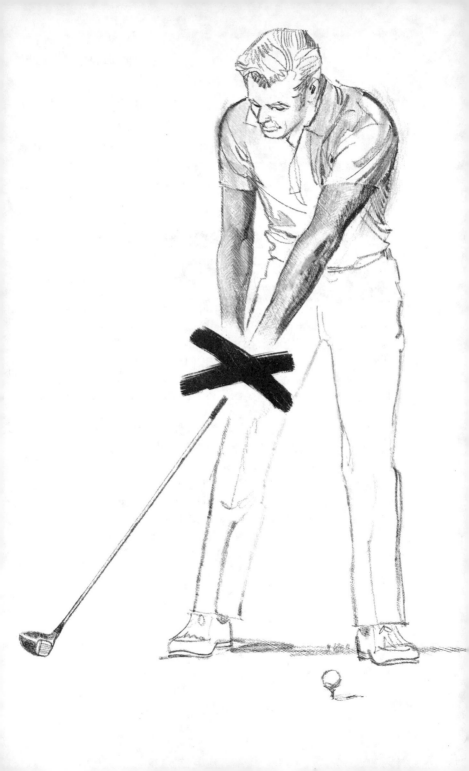

Take hands away from takeaway

For a smooth takeaway, you should have the sensation that you are moving the clubhead away from the ball with the arms and shoulders, not the hands.

Those who think of their hands at this critical stage often tighten their grip. This pushes the clubhead down, frequently causing it to catch in the grass behind the ball, closes the club-face and produces a wildly hooked shot. The added grip pressure also tightens the arms and shoulders, thus restricting the backswing.

—David L. Spencer

51

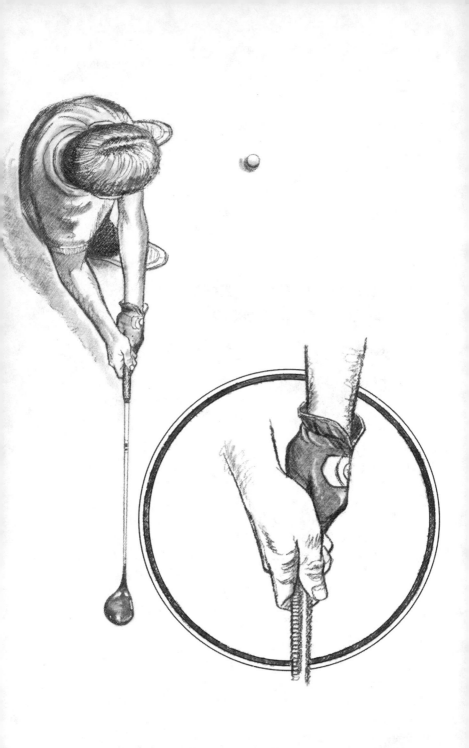

One-knuckle backswing keeps clubface square on target line

Many golfers have trouble swinging the club back straight and keeping the clubface on line. They roll or fan the club open on the takeaway, causing all kinds of errors. To keep the clubface on line, simply keep the back of the left hand straight as you swing the club away from the ball. An easy way to check this is to make sure that you can see just one knuckle at address and still only one as you swing the club back until it reaches waist-high. From that point, let your wrists break naturally as you complete your backswing.

—Johnny Palmer

Aim handle at ball to check plane

A sound swing has a good plane. An easy way to check your swing plane is to make sure the handle or grip end of your club points directly at the ball approximately halfway through the backswing and again on the downswing at about the same point.

If the handle points toward your toes, you're too upright. If it points outside the ball, you're too flat. If it's aiming directly at the ball, you have a swing that stays on the same plane from start to finish, requires no adjustments to get the clubface squarely on the ball and will consistently produce accurate shots. —*Lew Worsham*

Point to sky with proper turn

A proper backswing turn is made with the left shoulder and with very little manipulation of the clubhead with the hands. To make sure you are doing this correctly check the position of the clubhead when your hands are waist-high on the backswing. The toe should be pointing straight to the sky. If it is not, you have unconsciously over-manipulated your hands. If the blade is pointed left as you look at it, you've hooded the club. If the blade is pointing right, you've fanned it open.

—Bill Davis

57

Seniors: when left arm bends, you've swung back too far

When you get into the senior category and your bones start to creak a bit, accept the fact your swing will not be as full as it once was. Don't try to get the club back as far as you did in your younger days, because your swing will break down. A good gauge is to swing as far as you can and still keep your left arm straight—not rigid but reasonably straight. If the arm bends too much, you're overswinging. Now concentrate on swinging smoothly through the ball, resisting the temptation to "jump" at it because of your shorter swing. You may lose a little distance, but you will gain consistency.

—*Fred Horter*

59

FORWARD SWING

Cut your speed to add consistency

How hard should you swing at the golf ball? Usually with just 80 to 85 percent of your potential power. Swinging with reduced speed—within yourself, as the saying goes—helps in several ways: you strike the ball solidly for 18 holes, not just on the front nine, because you tire less readily; you play better under windy conditions; you always have some power in reserve when you need it. So find your best speed and swing every club in the bag at the same tempo, maintaining this tempo throughout the round. *—Don Pauley*

NO

Swing low for sweet shots

For the best iron-shot results the club-head should be swung into the ball on the same low angle that it took at the start of the backswing. The inevitable result of such a swing is a shallow divot in front of the ball's original position.

Many golfers, upon hearing that you must hit down on the ball, swing the clubhead into the ball on an angle too steep or abrupt. There is little chance of solidly hitting the back of the ball. But if the clubhead follows a low angle in the impact area, you will make sweet contact. —*Davis Love*

65

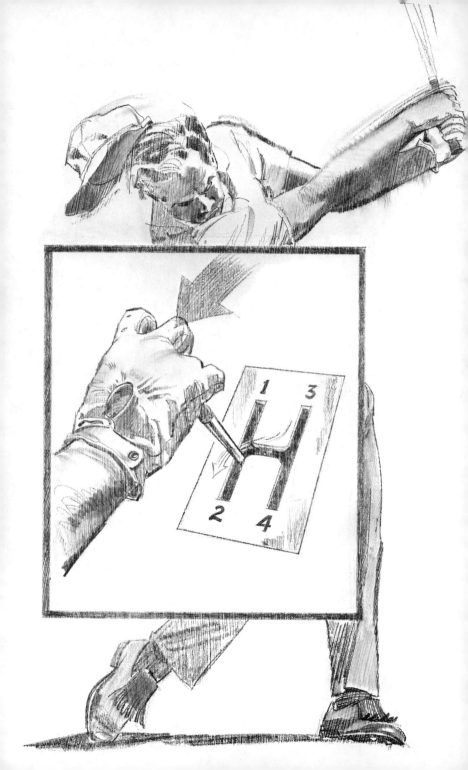

Throttle back to regain tempo

Whenever I feel my tempo and rhythm are off, and my shots begin to stray, I just make sure I'm not trying to over-power the ball. I slack off, just a little, from striving for distance. I think only of meeting the ball solidly. After a few holes of this semi-cautious play, once I'm hitting straight shots again, I'll gradually turn on the power I need to reach the par-5s in two and set up those money-winning birdies.

—*Lanny Wadkins*

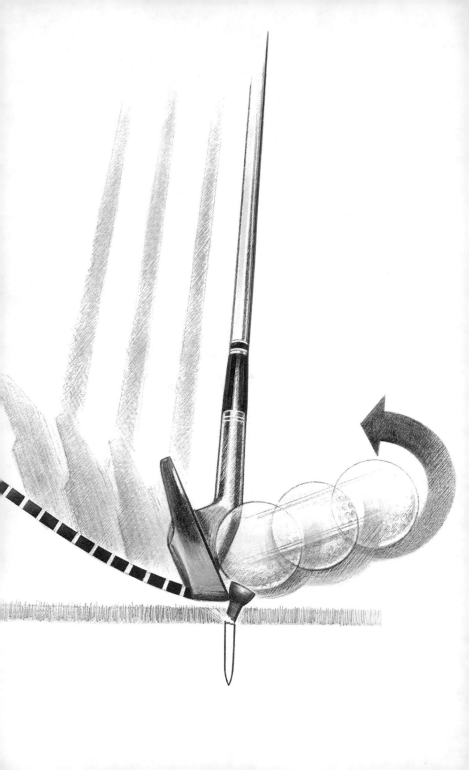

Break tee on par 3

When teeing off with an iron on par-3 holes the ball should be spun vertically so that it stays on line and stops rather quickly after landing on the green. To achieve this, think of breaking off the top of the tee under the ball at impact. It may not actually happen, since the ball should be teed quite low. But if you think of this you will swing so the clubhead contacts the ball while on a slightly downward path. Players who pick the ball cleanly off the tee are more likely to put sidespin on the ball, which will cause it to veer off line and run after it lands.

—Joseph F. Donadio

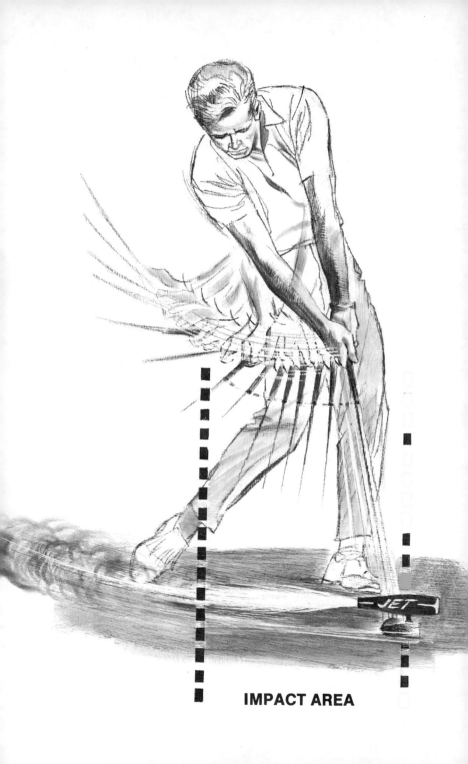

IMPACT AREA

'Free wheel' through ball to ease tension

Many golf shots are ruined because the player is uncertain about the outcome of the shot. He tenses up on the downswing, grabbing the club with a tightened grip in a conscious attempt to direct the ball on its way. I call this "pre-serving" the swing. It won't work.

To overcome this, I recommend that you "re-time" your downswing—that is, consciously do your utmost to move the clubhead rapidly through impact with a light grip and free-wheeling swing. Trust this thought to hit the ball, and you will be pleased with the result.

—*Bob Kletcke*

71

Practice karate to swing through ball

A karate expert psyches himself into believing that when he swings his hand through a stack of bricks or boards there will be absolutely no resistance from the object. He gains maximum speed from thinking of swinging through the object rather than at it. This same mental attitude is helpful in the golf swing. Gear your thinking to swinging the clubhead *through* the ball, and you will find your shots flying far and true.

—*Dave Walters*

Move ball back to stop hitting fat

Many golfers in the North get in the bad habit of hitting slightly behind the ball or "fat" with their irons. This shot, which makes the ball fly with less backspin, sometimes can be serviceable on lush northern fairways and greens. Unfortunately, this shot won't work in the South. It won't hold on the firm greens, and the hard fairways cause the clubhead to bounce, resulting in thin or topped shots. I recommend that a northern golfer who has this problem move the ball back in his stance about one inch and concentrate on hitting down and through the ball. An added benefit to this adjustment will be a lower trajectory to your shots, aiding your ball control in the strong southern winds.   —*Toby Brown*

Tunnel vision gives you straighter shots

Most weekend golfers see too much when they look at the shot facing them. Their peripheral vision takes in too wide a view of the hazards on the left or right of the fairway. Fear then takes over. If all you see is that lake on the right, that's probably just where you'll hit the shot.

Experienced players learn to have tunnel vision, seeing only the area where they want the shot to go. You should concentrate on where you want the ball to land and ignore the trouble.

—*Paul Bondeson*

Hit the ball over second base

Golfers often do not take time to get a clear picture in their minds of where they want their tee shots to go, which means they never can hit shots consistently down the center of the fairway. One way to do this is to picture a baseball diamond. Swing the club out toward second base as if you were cracking a hit up the middle. You'll find your tee shots will begin winding up in the center of the fairway.

—*Mike Smith*

Relax and release to cure shank

Many people have kidded me about my name, but rather than avoid me they invariably ask me how to cure shanking. One major cause of this dread affliction is tension—when the golfer worries about shot results he tries to steer the ball and fails to release his wrists and arms from their cocked position at the top of the backswing. So relax the grip and free up the muscles in the forearms, allowing the wrists to unhinge properly and the arms to roll over. If the rolling movement is done too quickly, it will cause the ball to fly to the left, but no shank will result and confidence will be restored. —*Craig Shankland*

Cast your lure to hit ball straight

Golfers often fail to release the clubhead properly through the ball. Fear of hitting the shot astray causes them to "block" their natural swing at impact. The usual result is that the shot goes right, because the clubface has not been squared. To free your muscles and produce straighter shots, think of the clubhead as a light fishing lure attached to the end of the clubshaft. You are going to send it flying toward your target. You'll find your clubface will end up square at the impact area.
—*Bert Weaver*

83

Knock over the cup to stop 'spinning shoulders'

Most golfers are plagued with an over-active right side at the start of the downswing. The cause of this error often is incorrectly diagnosed as "spinning shoulders." Actually, spinning shoulders are a symptom of poor footwork. Correct footwork encourages correct shoulder action. As a drill, place a paper cup four inches inside your right heel. As you begin your downswing slide your right heel into the cup and knock it over. By sliding your right heel you will cause your right shoulder to move correctly under your chin.   —*Don Silvanic*

Make hands win race with clubhead

Your hands and clubhead are accelerating like horses in a race as they cross the "finish line." Imagine a vertical line extending up from the ball which designates the impact point (or finish line) in the swing. Always be sure of two things in your swing. First, have your hands across the finish line before the clubhead. Second, accelerate as you cross the finish line. This will give you added power and improved direction.   —*Rick Hoover*

87

Give your leg drive some punch

Improper sequence of movements in the downswing is the ruination of many golf shots. Too often, players hit first with their hands and upper bodies instead of properly leading with their legs. If this is your problem, you can learn the feeling of proper sequence by addressing the ball without a club and imagining a punching bag hanging about three feet down the target line. Now throw an underhand punch with your right hand to the belly of the bag. To do this you'll have to stride to your left, which pulls along your torso and finally your shoulders, arm and hand as you release the punch at the last possible moment. This same sequence adapted to golf produces a more powerful swing.   —*Jack Clark*

Keep right foot square for square hit

Those seeking to improve accuracy should see that the right foot remains more or less perpendicular to the line of flight during the downswing. Pressure should be felt on the inside of the ball of the right foot. This helps keep the clubhead on a path that will approach the ball slightly from the inside and eventually produce a square hit.

A common fault is to let the right foot twist counterclockwise on the downswing. This forces the clubhead to swing into the ball from outside the target line and usually produces a slice. —*Bob Ledbetter*

91

Ladies: Keep knees alive for longer drive

Many women do not achieve their distance potential because they do not allow their legs to work properly on the forward swing. Clubhead speed is generated primarily by the arms, but for the arm swing to work most efficiently, the lower body must serve as a platform.

To accomplish this, there first must be a feeling of slight tension, an "aliveness," in the legs at address. Swing the arms back first, with the lower body following. This puts the lower body in position to lead the forward swing with a definite thrust of the knees toward the target, while the arms swing swiftly through impact. Learning to time this proper sequence of moves is the key to achieving good distance on your shots. —*Janice Phelps*

93

Sledge a wedge to feel your stroke

Golfers continually search for a model of what the swing should look and feel like. One of the most strikingly similar actions to a golf swing is that of driving a wedge into the base of a tree with a sledgehammer. This swing with a sledge teaches you proper feel in two vital areas: 1. it would be impossible to swing the sledge down without a weight shift, thus creating the proper left-side lead; 2. the radius created by the left arm must remain intact throughout the swing to insure accurate striking of the wedge.

—*Kenneth Green*

95

Keep head behind hip and let 'er rip

Keeping your upper body behind the ball on your downswing is a must if your clubhead is to reach maximum velocity through the impact area. If you let your shoulders slide toward the target, you destroy the centrifugal force that builds up this clubhead speed. Think of keeping your head behind your right hip until the club-head is well past the ball. This will encourage the proper sliding-turning action of the knees and hips and will discourage you from trying to hit the ball with the arms only. —*Sam Bacon*

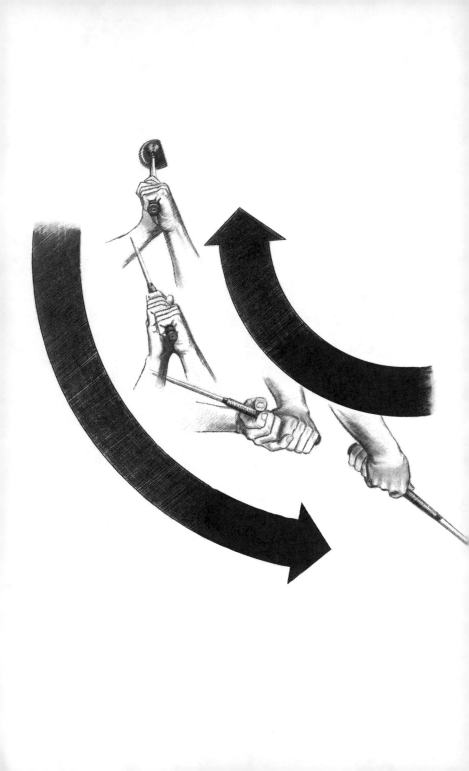

Keep hands square for square shots

To promote square striking and true shots you must keep the clubface square to the arc of your swing. Here's a thought that may help you do this: Keep your hands in the same relative position from address to the top of the backswing and back down to impact. If, at those three points, you can feel as though the hands have not moved or changed position in relation to your swing plane, then your clubface will strike the ball squarely and you can let the rest of your golf swing take care of itself. —*Ace Noonan*

99

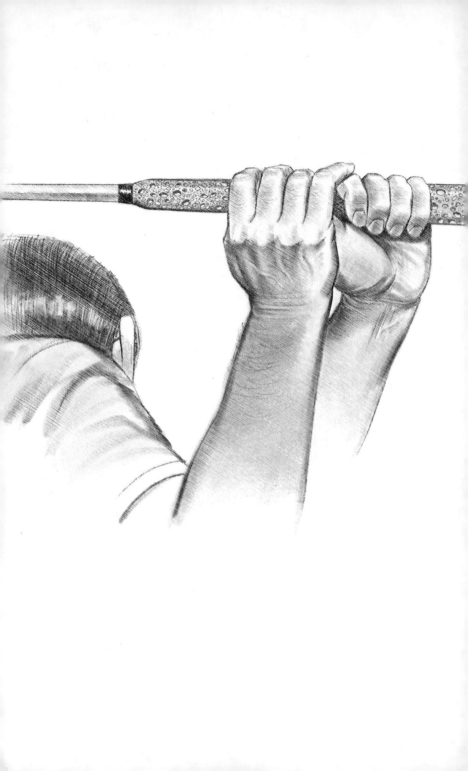

Grip a sponge for smoother swing

The golfer who plays infrequently tends to grip the club too tightly, especially at the top of the backswing. This tenses the muscles in the shoulders and upper body, forcing them to react too quickly at the start of the downswing. Often this causes the player to swing "over" the shot—outside the target line—and forces him to expend power before contact with the ball. It is important that the hands do not grab at the top. There should be a relaxed feeling that allows almost a pause before the body starts into the downswing. To achieve the proper feel and timing try relaxing your grip by imagining that the grip of the club is a wet sponge and you don't want to squeeze any water out. This relaxed grip at the top allows centrifugal force to take over on the downswing. It encourages the muscles to let the swing "just happen."—*Al Mengert*

101

Move your legs straight down the track

The lower body is recognized as a source of power in the golf swing, but it also serves as a transportation system for the arms and hands and as a guidance system for the clubshaft. You should have the feeling that you start your downswing by moving your legs straight down a line parallel to the target line. This will pull your arms and hands—and with them the shaft—directly down the intended line of flight. This is a movement you can practice indoors this winter and you'll be ahead when spring arrives.   *—Luca Barbato*

FINISH

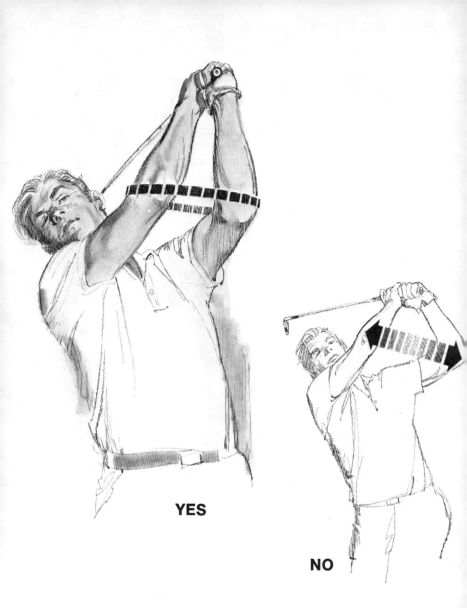

YES

NO

Finish with elbows tied together

At the finish of a full swing, your elbows should be reasonably close together. Striving for this type of finish naturally promotes the correct squaring-up of the clubface at impact. Chronic slicers often allow their elbows to spread apart during the swing, which causes the clubface to slide across the ball, producing that ugly sidespin. —*Jerry Bass*

107

Point belt buckle at target

The way a golfer finishes his shot tells me a great deal about his swing. If he has hit *at* the ball rather than *through* the ball, chances are that most of his swing arc was backswing and too little was follow-through. His weight probably did not shift properly to his left side on his downswing and he did not complete a full turn of body and hips. Thus he probably blocked out with his hips, or inhibited his hand action.

To encourage my pupils to hit through the ball, I tell them to follow through until their belt buckle points to the target. This forces their weight over onto their left side, and turns and clears the left side out of the way so that the clubhead can accelerate through the ball. At the finish the hands should be high and there should be just enough weight on the right foot to maintain proper balance.

—*Vernon Harwell*

'Pose' at finish to find your balance

An effective way to improve your balance throughout your swing is to pretend that you're going to be photographed at the finish. If you can "pose" for several seconds at this point, you will have swung in good balance. This produces a repeating swing and, in turn, consistent shotmaking. If you "totter" at the finish, your balance is faulty. —*Richard Mackey*

SLICING

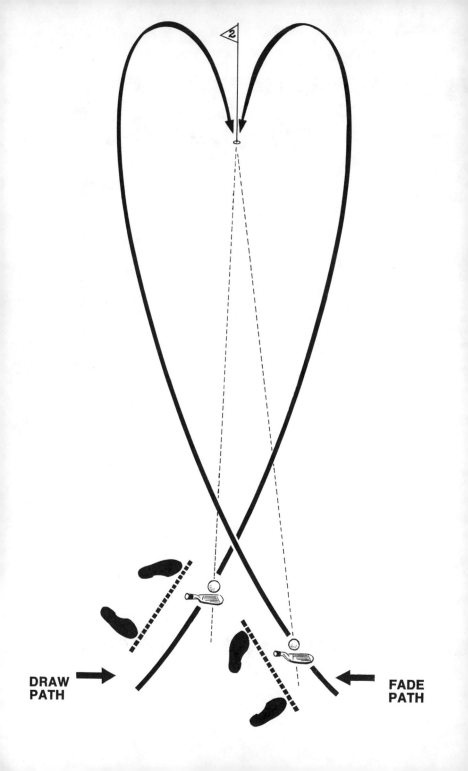

DRAW
PATH

FADE
PATH

Angle of attack determines direction of shot

For a controlled fade the clubhead must approach the ball from outside the target line and reach impact with the clubface "looking" at the target. This imparts clockwise spin to the ball, which will start left and then turn right.

To induce this clubhead path, stand so that a line across your toes would extend to the left of the target. This will encourage your swinging the clubhead along a parallel line.

To hit the intentional draw, merely reverse the procedure. Set up so you'll swing the clubhead across the target line from inside to outside. If your clubface is looking at the target during impact, it will apply the counterclockwise spin you need to make the shot curve gently from right to left.

—*Ken Towns*

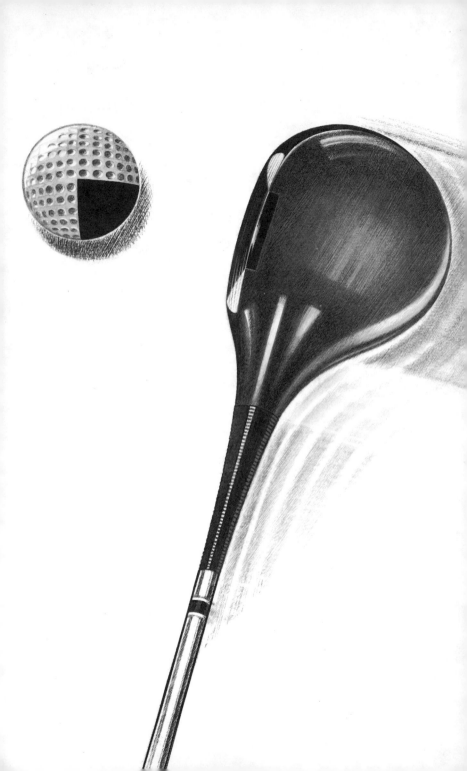

Aim at this slice of the ball to stop slicing

If you are troubled with slicing or pulling the ball, it usually means you are "coming over the top"—swinging the clubhead through the ball from outside to inside the target line. Try this mental imagery. As you address the ball imagine that it is divided into quarter sections. Think of swinging the club into the inside back quarter of the ball. Then your clubhead will take a downswing path from inside the target line to along it. Your shots will straighten out and you may even develop a little right-to-left draw.   —*Frank Beard*

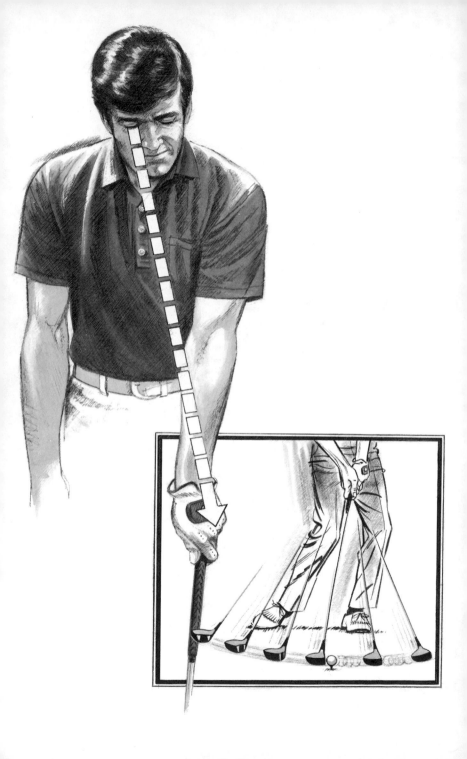

Right hand crosses over left to correct slice

If you've sliced all your golfing life, this tip is for you. Slicers never experience the sensation of the right hand crossing over the left on the downswing. To achieve this feeling, close your left eye and take your left-hand grip so that you can see four knuckles on your left hand. Open your eyes and place your right hand on the club so you can see one knuckle. Take a swing and try to make the toe of the club pass the heel as soon as possible in the downswing. By hitting balls this way you will end your slicing days forever. As you become more proficient at hooking the ball you can move your grip back to a more normal position.   —*Eric Monti*

119

NO

To straighten out slice, turn shoulders

If you slice the ball you probably need a better shoulder turn. A correct shoulder turn encourages a correct inside-to-down-the-line swing path. To acquire the feeling of a good shoulder turn, place the ball in your stance so that a line drawn vertically from the ball would intersect the outside portion of your left shoulder. On your backswing, turn your upper body so that both shoulders are behind this line instead of swaying toward the target with your upper body. The proper shoulder position promotes a correct downswing, where the legs lead and the arms and shoulders follow. —*Jim Langley*

121

Combat slice with tennis 'forehand'

Chronic slicers often suffer from incorrect hand action at impact. Because they sometimes assume that the outer edge, rather than the back, of the left hand should lead the club through the ball, they never square the clubface to the target.

Actually, the *back* of the left hand, not the heel, should be looking and moving toward the target before, during and, for a time, after impact. A slicer can eventually reach this position if he will at first do some overcompensating.

Think of how the tennis forehand shot is made. The hand and arm brings the racquet "up and over" the ball. To overcome the slice in golf, use your hands similarly. Feel as if you are trying to turn your wrists over quickly after contact. This will square the face and produce a straighter shot.

—*Gene Shields*

123

CHIPPING AND PITCHING

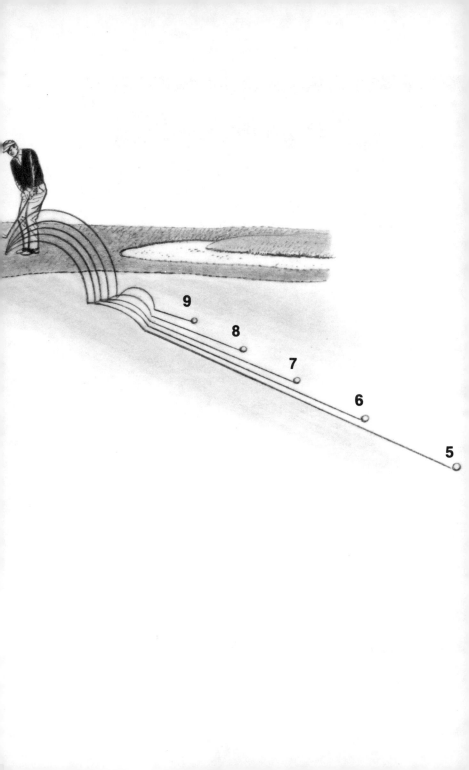

Distance dictates club choice for chip shots

Becoming proficient with the chip shot is the easiest way for the high handicap golfer to lower his scores. The commonest fault inexperienced players commit is to use the same club, regardless of the amount of putting surface they must cover to reach the flagstick.

The general rule to follow is: the more distance to the flagstick, the less loft you should take. An easy way to prove this to yourself is to lay the 5-, 6-, 7-, 8- and 9-irons in a row along the edge of the practice green. Place five balls about three feet from the green and, starting with the 5-iron, chip to a spot three feet on the green. Hit each iron, in order, with the same stroke to the same spot, noticing the difference in the run of the balls. Good chippers use the club that will best get the job done with the least chance for error.

—Felice Torza

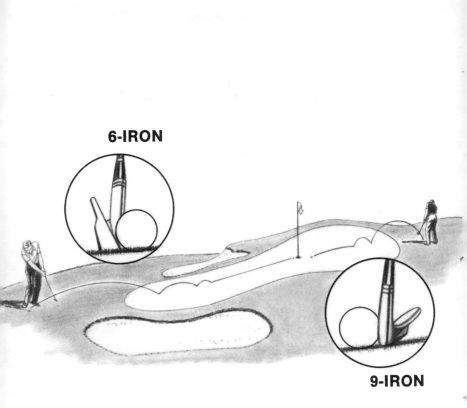

6-IRON

9-IRON

Chip low going uphill, high coming down

Using the same club for every chip shot, contrary to what many golfers believe, will not necessarily build consistency or accuracy. In fact, it can cost many strokes that otherwise might be saved. Most good chippers use the proper club for each different situation and have no favorites.

In most cases the ball should be carried just onto the putting surface on the fly, thereafter bouncing and rolling to the hole. To accomplish this when playing uphill to the green, a running shot should be played with a 5-, 6- or 7-iron to keep the ball low and allow it to land with a minimum of backspin. Going downhill, the ball should be hit higher, with an 8, 9 or wedge. These more lofted clubs will give enough height and backspin to help check the ball when it hits the downslope.

—Bob Spence

Hit chip shots low for truer roll

It is much easier to gauge how much a chip shot will roll if the ball is struck solidly, with as little backspin as possible. Therefore I recommend using the straighter-faced 4-, 5- and 6-irons, rather than clubs of more loft which often either "blade" the ball over the green or backspin it so much that the shot stops well short of the cup.

To encourage solid contact with these clubs, imagine that there is a tack imbedded directly into the back of the ball. The idea is to tap the tack smartly with wrists firm. You will put less backspin on the shot and drive the ball directly forward and on line.

—Ernie Schneiter

131

Maintain the triangle for consistent chips

Many chips are missed because a player tries to lift the ball in the air by scooping with the right hand. The common result is to skull the ball across the green or to hit it fat. To end scooping, imagine that your arms and shoulders form a triangle, with the club an extension of your left arm. Maintain the triangle during the chip shot by using little or no wrist action. The clubhead's loft will propel the ball into the air and you will strike the ball crisply and more consistently.   —*DeDe Owens*

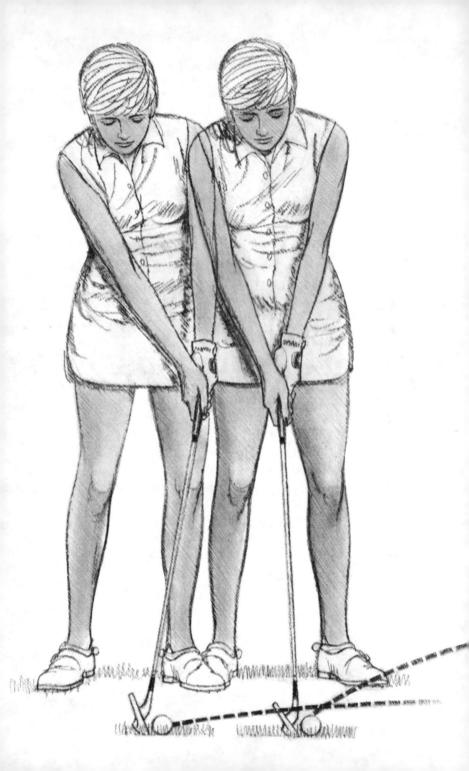

Move hands to change chipping trajectory

To control the trajectory of your short chip shots (about five yards from the edge of the green on in) merely alter the position of your hands at address. There is no need to change the position of the ball. If you want a low trajectory, so the ball will roll more readily, move your hands well ahead of the ball, over your left foot. This takes effective loft off the clubface. If you want a higher, or more normal trajectory, to land the ball closer to the hole, position your hands only an inch or so ahead of the ball. I like to use the same club for all chips. The one in which I have the most confidence is the 8-iron.

—*Chris Repasky*

135

Use putter chop for buried chip

Balls which bury in lush fringe areas around the green present a special shot-making problem. The heavy bent grass tends to grab the club on normal pitches or chips, causing a "fat" shot. To avoid this, select a putter, play the ball well back toward the right foot and position your hands well ahead of the ball at address. Then simply hinge your wrists, cocking the club away from the ball in a steep upward arc, then *drop* the putterhead onto the back of the ball. Avoid any follow-through. The ball will pop up with a high hop topspin, carrying it over the fringe and onto the green toward the hole.

Remember, the length of the backswing is the determining factor in how far the ball will go. A nominal amount of practice will give you a feel for this and soon you'll be saving strokes in a surefire way. *—Francis Keenan*

Clamp your right elbow in for chipping control

All chip shots should be made with the right elbow tucked in reasonably close to the right side. Do not allow the elbow to move away from the side even after impact. Imagine that it is clamped to your side. This will enable you to control the clubhead more consistently.

—*Joe M. Durgan*

Firm wrists for short wedge-chip

Firm wrists are especially important on short wedge-chip shots from heavy grass. Thick grass, by wrapping around the hosel, tends to close the clubface at impact and force the shot to the left. Only firmness in the wrists will prevent this from happening.

Take a couple of practice swings near the ball to test the exact resistance of the grass. Then take a short backswing and try to move the club crisply into the back of the ball. Let the clubhead swing out along the line toward the target with wrists still firm.

—*Lew Worsham*

141

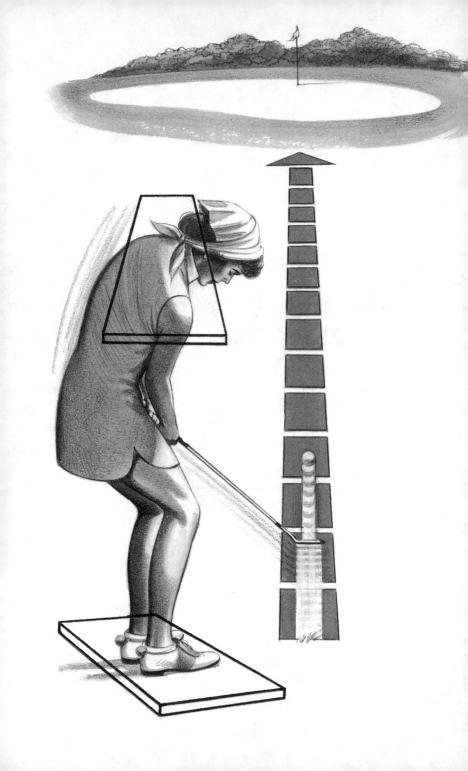

Open stance but square shoulders for short shots

When hitting chips and short pitch shots your stance should be open. You can see the target better and move your body out of the way more easily. But if your shoulders fall too far open, poor shots can result. Your swing will go left of target. Take your normal open stance, then rotate your shoulders so they are square, or parallel to the target line. You'll feel a slight stretching in the lower left portion of your back. Swing your arms along your shoulder line. The force of your swing will be toward the target instead of to the left. *—Jan Wood*

Imagine lob to elevated green

Imagination plays an important role in determining how fully to hit a fairway wedge shot to an elevated green.

To get a sense of how far to take your club back, imagine tossing the ball underhanded in a high lob toward the green, and picture as your target a bushel basket on the green. The basket image is useful in picturing the kind of high shot needed to hit, and stay on, an elevated green.

Visualizing the shot in this way will give you a precise feeling for the amount of force you need in your swing with the wedge. Just take the club back with the same force and movement in mind and you will be able to go for the green with confidence.

—*John Jurus*

145

Land your shots 'on the stick'

Most average golfers usually finish short of the hole on full approach shots with the pitching wedge. To encourage shooting all the way to the cup, I suggest they visualize the ball landing on top of the flagstick, rather than in front of the hole. This practice, though admittedly a gimmick, engenders a combination of boldness and good timing that results in an increased number of one-putt possibilities.

—*Mike Caraway*

147

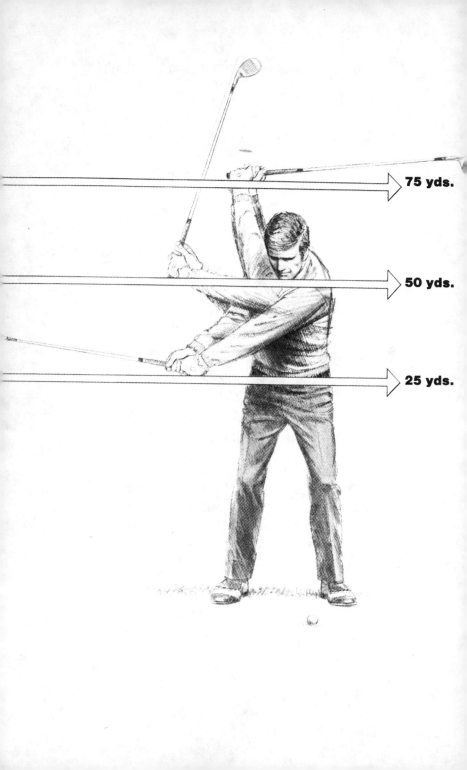

75 yds.

50 yds.

25 yds.

Let backswing control length of wedge shots

If you are not sure how hard to hit a wedge a given distance, and most golfers are not, you should bring your backswing into the computation. For most golfers, from a normal lie, a 75-yard shot requires swinging your hands back head high—virtually a full swing —and striking the ball a firm blow. For a 50-yard shot, take it back shoulder high; for a 25-yarder, swing back hip high. This, of course, can vary somewhat with the individual. Find out on the practice tee your own tendencies —swing back hip high and measure from there, for example—and enter them into your personal computer. Then you can approach the shot with confidence. —*Gene Shields*

149

Keep left leg quiet for pitch-shot balance

Those who allow the left knee to point well behind the ball during the backswing on short pitch shots will have difficulty staying in balance and probably will scuff the shot.

To maintain balance through the 50-yard wedge shot, try maintaining an almost motionless—but not rigid—left leg through the backswing. A line from the top of the leg through the knee should point an inch or so in front of the ball from address through impact. To do this you must start with most of your weight to the left and leave it there as you swing.

For such a shot your hands need move only to shoulder-height at the top of the backswing and to the same height at the finish.   —*John Austin*

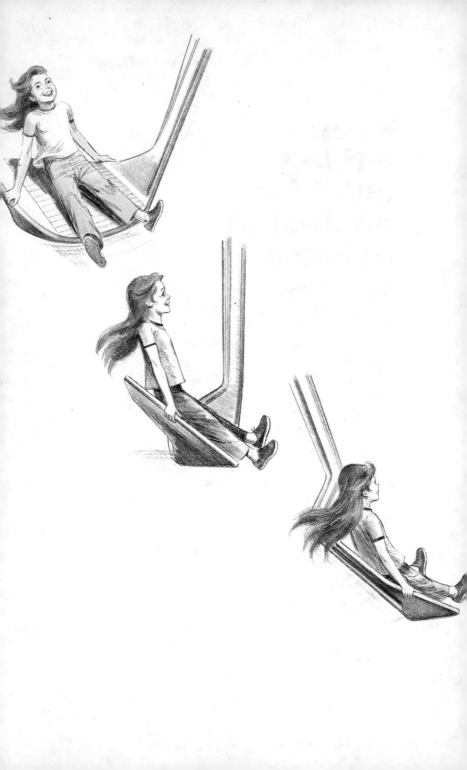

Swing the child on short pitch shots

Poor wedge play around the greens is invariably caused by poor tempo and clubhead manipulation by your hands. Next time you have a wedge pitch of 10 to 15 yards, imagine a child sitting in a backyard swing. As you bring the club back and through, picture the face of your wedge holding that youngster. Don't turn your hands abruptly or the child will fall out. Swing the club on a straight path to the target and watch your pitch shots improve.

—*Joanne Winter*

'Ghost' clubhead under ball for high, soft pitch

A shot often missed by golfers is one requiring a short, high pitch over a hazard to a small, fast green. The shot must rise steeply but softly and with little spin to settle quickly. This requires a delicate, gentle swing in which no particular force is applied to the ball (providing your lie is decent). Using a light pitching wedge, preferably with little flange, play the ball forward in an open, narrow stance, open the clubface and position your hands slightly behind the ball. Take a nearly full backswing with little wrist-break and slide or "ghost" the clubhead under the ball. It's almost as if you're not touching the ball at all. —*Mac Hunter*

SAND PLAY

YES

NO

Take shallow cut from powdery sand

Soft, powdery sand frustrates many golfers. The club blade cuts too deeply and takes too much sand, which causes the ball to finish short.

To escape from powdery sand, open the club blade slightly at address so that it faces a little to the right of target. If you play the ball forward, opposite your left foot, the opened face will "ride through" the sand readily, taking a shallow cut, instead of digging downward abruptly. Keep your left arm firm throughout the swing and try to finish with your hands extended out toward the hole. —*Sam Drake*

159

Open face from buried lie

Traditional teaching tells us to hood the face for a buried lie in the sand. This extricates the ball from the sand but has the disadvantage of flying the ball on a low trajectory with little or no backspin. Often the ball rolls far past the hole with this method. To keep from overrunning the hole, try opening the face and setting your hands slightly ahead of the ball at address. Take the club back a bit more upright than usual and try to drop the club in the sand just behind the "rim" of the lie. The ball comes out on a higher trajectory and will not roll so far.

—*Butch Liebler*

Swing a beach pail in the sand

Many sand shots fail because of a hurried swing. Golfers who are afraid of leaving the ball in the sand, or over-hitting the green altogether, unconsciously speed up their swings. This destroys timing and causes inconsistency.

I instruct my pupils to pretend that they are swinging a bucket full of water. To swing the bucket back and forth without spilling a drop, tempo must be smooth and unrushed. As they establish this tempo through a bit of practice, they dramatically improve their control of sand shots.

—*Gloria Armstrong*

163

Sweep ball from fairway trap

One of the most difficult shots in golf is the fairway bunker shot, where you need a full swing with a less lofted club to reach the green. A common fault is to try to strike the ball with a downward swing path. If you hit just a fraction behind the ball, the shot is ruined.

Instead, envision yourself sweeping the ball off the sand. Concentrate on controlling the club with your left hand and side, make a smooth takeaway and swing through toward your target. Play the ball back toward your right foot an inch or so to make sure you catch the ball first. There's no need to try to lift or dig the ball out . . . or even to touch the sand at all. The loft of the club will do the work for you as you sweep the ball away.   —*Gary Ellis*

Splash sand like water

Remember how you used to splash a friend in a pool by flipping your hand through the surface of the water? That's the same clubhead action needed to make a successful shot from sand. You should take a shallow cut from under the ball with an open clubface. Then just splash.

—*Ed Griffiths*

PUTTING

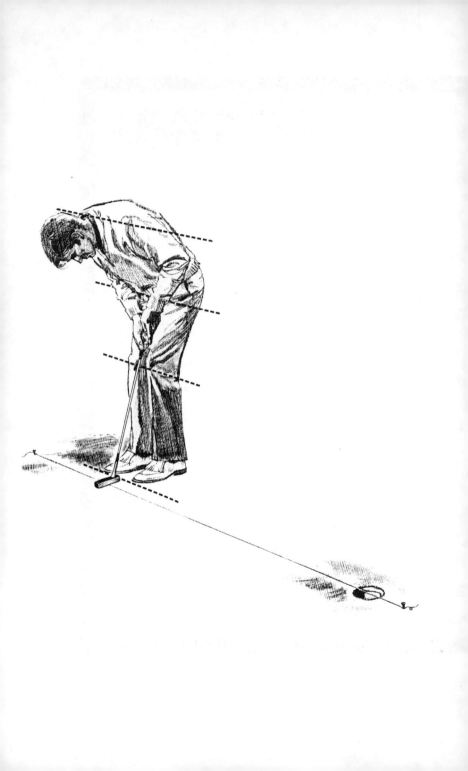

Set yourself for on-line stroke

I've found that most golfers can determine the line of a putt with relative ease. But they frequently run into trouble because they fail to align their bodies with the line they've chosen. They misalign themselves to left or right of target and, as a natural result, misdirect the putterhead in that direction.

Take a 10-foot piece of string and "tack" one end of it behind a hole on the putting green with a wooden tee. Extend the string directly over the hole to your ball. Then practice aligning your feet, hips and shoulders parallel to the string, and swinging the putter toward the hole. This drill will soon give you a feeling for setting up square to your intended line. In no time you will eliminate any pushing or pulling of putts caused by improper body alignment.   —*Lou Garrison*

171

Improve rhythm with a simple stroke

Timing and rhythm are important in all phases of one's golf game but especially in putting, where rushing your stroke and thus pushing or pulling the ball off line is just as costly as whiffing a tee shot. To retain good timing and rhythm on your putts, avoid concentrating on the mechanics of the stroke during actual play. Such thoughts as taking it back with your right hand, or keeping the blade on line, complicate your stroke and destroy timing and rhythm. Instead, merely swing the putter back and forward smoothly, rhythmically—and simply.

—*Steve Huggins*

173

To stop 'stabs' make putter pass left shoe

A common ruination of a putt is the short stab, particularly under pressure. To lengthen and smooth out your stroke, try this approach. Widen your stance to about 20 inches, point the left foot out slightly and play the ball just inside the left heel. Then concentrate on making the putter blade pass the left toe on the forward stroke.

—*Pat O'Brien*

175

Stroke putter like a pool cue

The cardinal concept of putting to me is that you must take the putter away from the ball low and slow. That may not be quite grammatical, but I guarantee you it will work. Think of swinging the head of the putter back on the same path as you would a pool cue, low and almost parallel to the table. Don't jerk the putter up and away from the ball if you want to achieve a smooth, firm stroke.   —*Frank Beard*

177

Keep the same beat on all putts

Watch any great player and you'll notice that the rhythm of his putting stroke is the same, whether he putts a three-footer or a 60-footer. He swings the putter faster at impact on the 60-footer because his swing is longer, but the relationship between his backswing and forward swing is the same as on the three-footer. If you have difficulty judging distance on putts, you probably vary the rhythm of your stroke. Your putting stroke should be like a metronome; the tempo (speed) can vary but the rhythm or beat must be consistent. Let the length of your putting stroke roll the ball to the hole instead of striking it with a jerky "hit."
—*Mark Kizziar*

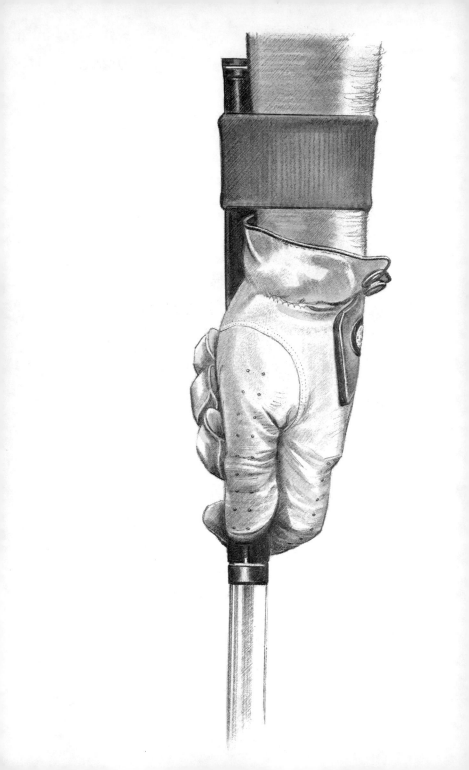

Band your wrist to practice a firmer putting stroke

One of the keys to consistently good putting is preventing your left wrist from breaking down or cupping during the stroke. As an aid in establishing this firm stroke, grip down on the putter handle and clamp the grip end to the inside of your left forearm with an elastic band. An ordinary tennis sweatband will do nicely. Then if the grip end pulls away from your arm during the stroke, you'll know your left wrist is breaking and you can work to correct it.

—*Peter Kostis*

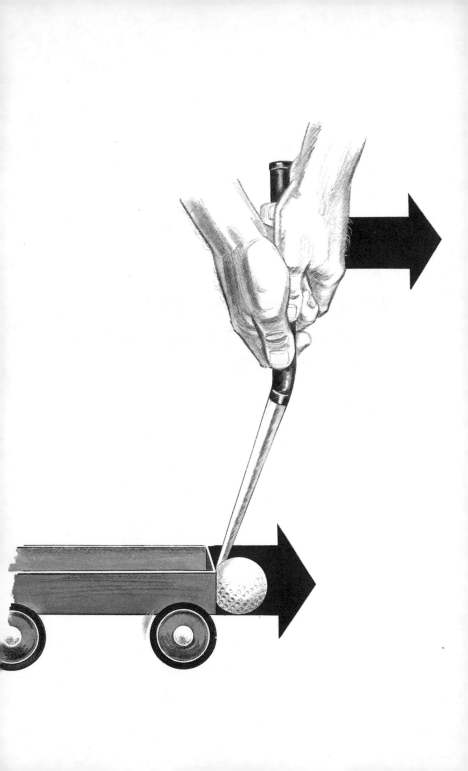

Pull your putter to make your putts

Since it is easier to pull an object straight than it is to push it, the putt should be stroked with a pulling motion of the left hand. Simply place the left hand slightly ahead of the putterhead at address. Make sure the left hand and putterhead stay in that relationship on the backswing. On the forward stroke, feel that the back of the left hand is stable and is moving squarely toward the target as it pulls the clubhead along behind it. This will keep your putterblade—and your putts —square and on line.

—*Richard D. Gordin*

Squeeze knees inward for steady putting

Movement of the body during the stroke is a common cause of poor putting. This usually is caused by an unsteady body position. All great putters, no matter what their style, maintain a fixed center during the stroke.

One excellent way to accomplish this is to squeeze your knees inward, toward each other, exerting just a slight tautness to keep them in place—as if you were holding a balloon between your knees. This centers your weight between your feet and prevents body movement by effectively "locking" you into place. —*Bill Hunter*

185

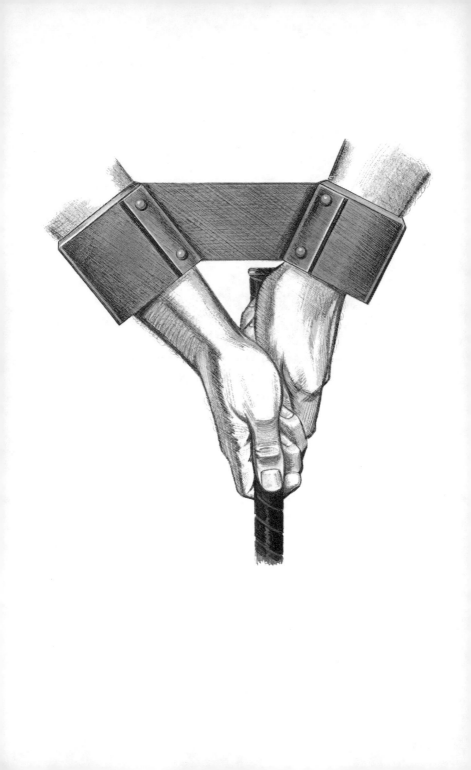

Wrists of the world, unite and putt!

One key to good putting is unity between the two hands during the stroke. A poor grip which causes one hand to dominate can destroy this unity. A simple thought to keep the hands working together is to feel that the wrists are close together at address and remain that way during the stroke. If you feel your wrists moving apart, your hand action probably is faulty.

—*Toby Lyons*

187

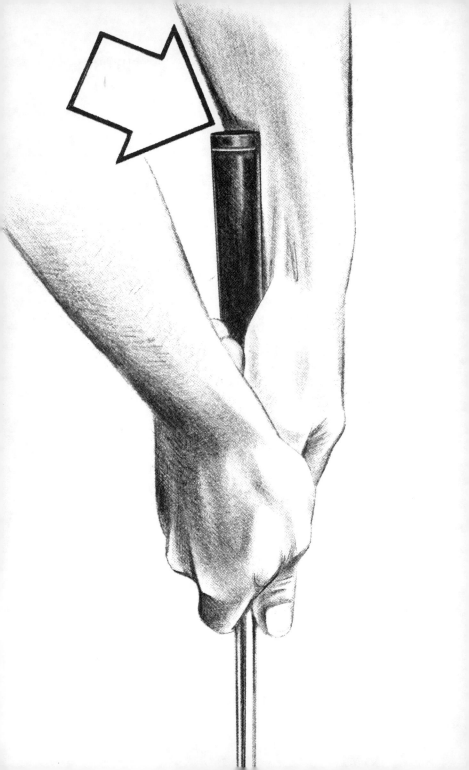

Shorten grip to firm up putting

Most poor putters suffer from over-active hands and wrists. Their left wrist breaks down at impact. Wristy putters suffer especially on long putts because they never know how solidly they are going to contact the ball. If a golfer comes to me with a wristy putting stroke, I have him shorten down on his grip so that he can press the handle end of the putter against his left forearm during the stroke. He must make his putting stroke without ever letting the handle end lose contact with his left forearm.

By practicing this drill he soon understands the feeling of an arms-and-shoulders stroke instead of a hands-and-wrists action. When he takes his normal grip I tell him to keep the same feeling he had during the drill.

—*Red Jessup*

Putt in a vacuum

Unless you can close your mind to outside distractions, you'll never putt up to your potential. Once I decide on the line and force needed for a putt, I try to feel as if I'm putting in a vacuum. No sound can penetrate it, and the only thought I allow is that of stroking the ball into the cup. —*Betsy Cullen*

Chart the break from afar

To help solve those rolls on the green, take a look at the putting surface in relation to the surrounding area while you are as far away as possible. Note the tilt of the green in relation to any vertical references available—buildings, telephone poles or trees. This will give you a better idea of the overall slope of the putting surface, often difficult to detect close up.

—*Doyle Manor*

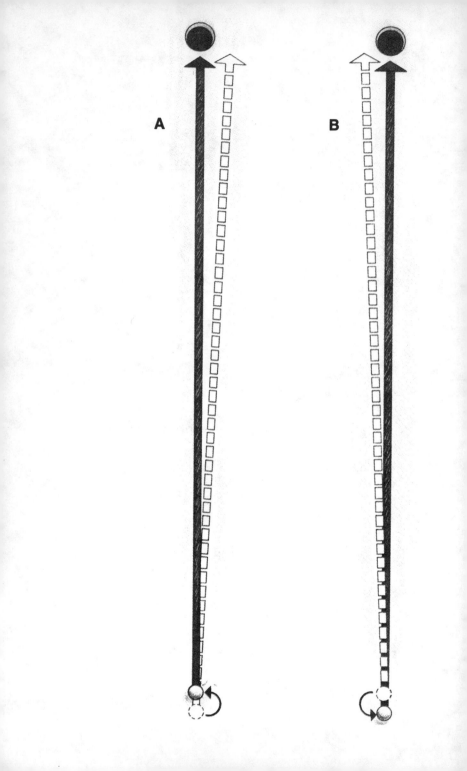

A   B

Align your putts with long-range practice

Five minutes of practice on long putts before a round will help any golfer's score. Even the best players' putting strokes change from day to day, and you are smart to detect possible errors before you tee off. Select the longest and straightest putts on the practice clock. After a few moments, you might see that you are missing consistently to one side or the other.

(A) If you are missing to the right, move the ball an inch or so toward your left foot. (B) If you are missing to the left, move the ball toward the right foot. This repositioning should correct your misalignment on short as well as long putts. —*John Bass*

195

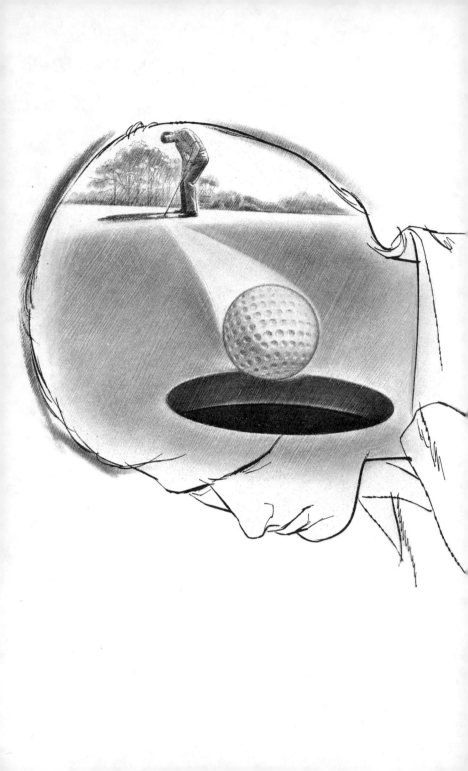

'See' the ball into the hole

The best way to help your putting is to allow your subconscious reflexes to take over by letting your eyes "tell" your fingers how to stroke the ball.

Line up your putt, take your stance, look at the hole, then look at the ball and putt without any further mental gymnastics. Trust what your eyes have seen, and you will putt well.

Try this to prove the validity of eye-finger coordination. Glance at a pencil on your desk. Look away, and reach for the pencil. Nine times out of 10 you'll pick up the pencil and you won't even have to think about it. The same thing works in putting. —*Nick Chillemi*

197

SPECIALTY SHOTS

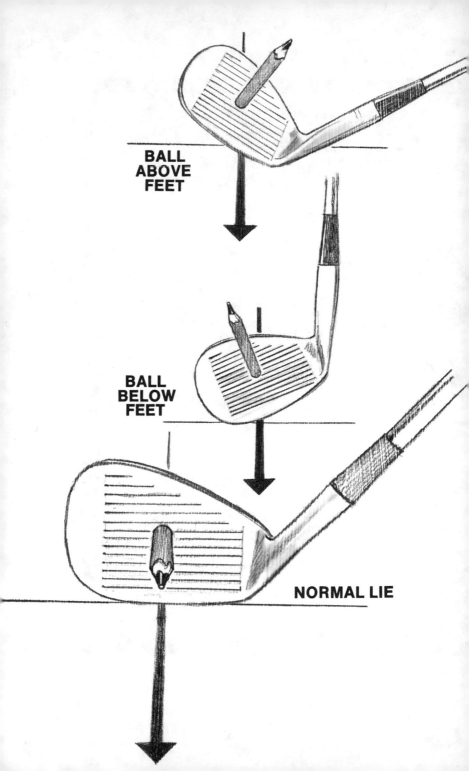

BALL ABOVE FEET

BALL BELOW FEET

NORMAL LIE

Sidehill lies: change aim, not swing

Sidehill lies cause problems for almost all golfers. When the ball lies above his feet, a right-hander will tend to pull it to the left. If it sits below his feet, he will probably push it to the right. As mysterious as this phenomenon sounds, it is readily explainable.

Suppose a ball were suspended in the air about waist high and you hit it, baseball style, with a wedge. Instead of rising and flying straight out, the ball would be pulled to the left. The loft of the wedge would aim the clubface off your left shoulder, not at the target. To some extent this happens on all shots when the ball is higher than your feet.

As a general rule, the ball will always tend to fly "downhill," in the direction of the slope. Instead of changing your swing to compensate for this factor, I recommend you simply allow for it by aiming higher up the hill.

—*Chuck Johnson Jr.*

Avoid turning a mistake into a disaster

To score well, you must learn to take the shot that *minimizes,* not accentuates, a previous error.

Let's say you slice your tee shot into the woods. You find yourself with a choice of two shots: (1) You can go for the green by making a superb shot through a narrow opening in the trees, or, (2) you can play directly out and into a fairway position that is well short of the green, but that permits a relatively easy third shot to the target.

The percentage player chooses the second alternative. It wasn't a good shot that put the ball in the woods. Why expect a great shot to get it out?

—*Paul Bumann*

Stymied by a tree? Aim right at it!

Being stymied behind a dense forest of trees is a common experience at many courses. In stroke play, caution to avoid a major disaster usually suggests playing safely out to the fairway. However, limited liability in match play— you may lose one hole, but not an irreversible number of shots—can make gambling worthwhile.

If just one tree trunk blocks a good escape route, and the tree is at least 20 yards from your ball and not too thick, I suggest you consider aiming right at it. You will probably miss the tree. Remember, a successful escape from trouble can often prove to be the turning point of a close match.

—*Frank Thacker*

Break down
distance on
strange course

Club selection can be an aggravating problem when playing away from home. On a flat course in the desert or in Florida, remember that your target usually looks farther away than it actually is. Pick out a tree or mound between you and the green, estimate how far it is to that object, then figure how far it is from the object to the green. By adding the two figures you should have a rough approximation of of the total yardage.

Conversely, in the mountains everything appears closer than it really is. Don't look at the mountains. Concentrate only on the flag. The flagstick can be deceiving but looking at the flag itself will give you good depth perception.   —*Mike Souchak*

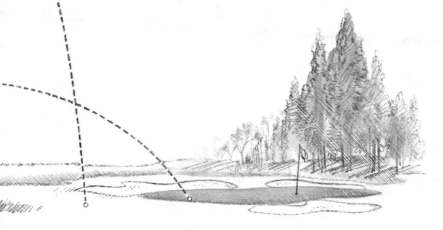

Close face slightly from Bermuda rough

The Bermuda rough in the South makes the ball pop straighter up in the air than northern rough. This causes many wedge shots to fall short. Close the clubface slightly at address. Use firm wrist action and follow through. You will get a more consistent shot, one with a lower trajectory and more run.
—*Eddie Bush*

209

Lofted woods solve long-iron woes

If the long irons are difficult for you to play, try adding a 6- and 7-wood to your bag. These eventually may become standard clubs for the average player, because they enable you to strike the ball farther and with less effort than the long irons. They are especially useful out of the rough, from tight lies and from downhill lies. Simply play the clubs as you would your 5-iron. Because they are higher lofted and give the shot so much backspin, you'll find they hold the greens better than long irons. The only time to beware of using them is when you are playing into a strong headwind.

—*Hubby Habjan*

Reduce your swing against the wind

One of the big problems in playing into the wind is pressing, trying to hit the ball too hard. This results in mis-hit shots, and the wind accentuates the errors. Think of taking only a half swing. Acquire the feeling that you are taking your hands only waist-high on the backswing. They actually will be going back farther than that, but this concept will help you keep your swing more compact, giving you more control to strike the ball squarely.

—*Jo Ann Prentice*

YES

NO

Bang down on ball to beat wind

Wind tunnel tests have shown that the type of shot least affected by a cross-wind is one that flies low with a lot of backspin. This shot is especially valuable on par-3 holes, where many golfers normally tend to pick the ball cleanly off the wooden tee and produce a floating shot that is really at the mercy of the wind.

To make these tee shots fly lower and backspin more, I simply tee the ball low, so it's all but sitting on the grass, and play it an inch or two farther back in my stance while keeping my hands well forward. Then I merely bang down on the back of the ball, wipe out the tee and take a little turf. The ball flies low and true.

—*Sandra Post*

215

Pick imaginary target in crosswind

Crosswinds are difficult to handle, especially on seaside courses. To combat them, visualize an imaginary flag left or right of the pin depending on the wind's direction. Take one more club than you would normally use and swing with a three-quarter effort. This will flight the ball low under the wind. Hit toward the imaginary flag without trying to manipulate the ball in any way —the wind will naturally push it to the target. *—Tom Riordan*

Swing slower in cold weather

Golfers who play during the winter months would be well advised to swing much easier than normal. It is natural to sense that the elements are something to overpower, but you should avoid the tendency to hit harder in wind and cold. Swinging too fast is bad under any conditions, but fatal in winter when bulkier clothes tend to restrict movement and cold temperatures cause muscles to tighten.

Prepare yourself mentally for an easy, rhythmic, flowing swing. Then make a conscious effort to take the club away slower than usual on your backswing.   —*Tommy Shannon*

Putt with wedge from heavy fringe

One of the most difficult shots in golf is the delicate chip from heavy fringe around the green. If you attempt to hit the shot normally, you run the risk of catching too much grass and hitting it "fat" or of putting unwanted spin on the ball that can throw it off line. A better alternative is to putt the ball with a sand wedge, assuming your normal putting grip and stance and aiming your stroke so you will hit the belly or equator of the ball with the leading edge of the club. This deliberate topping action will cause the ball to skip out of the heavy grass and roll true toward the hole. It will require some practice to gain confidence in the shot, but it will pay off in the long run.

—*Bob Hamrich*

PRACTICE DRILLS

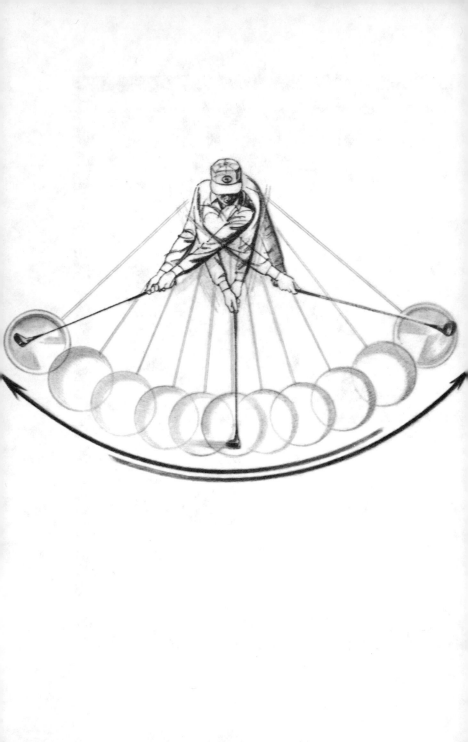

Warm up for round with pendulum drill

Proper warm-up before every round is essential to scoring well on the early holes. Here is a 60-second warm-up that you can use if you don't have more time or more elaborate facilities.

Using a driver, or whatever club you plan to swing on the first tee, take your normal stance and center your head over an imaginary ball. With your grip relaxed, swing the club back and forth continuously in the rhythm of a grandfather clock pendulum—not too fast, not too slow. Continue until you feel a rhythmic pattern.

About a minute of this drill is equal to hitting 30 balls on the range.

—*John Geertsen*

225

Swing blind to see errors

Golfers usually find it difficult to visualize just what they are doing in the swing, which is important if they are to correct a certain error. There is a way to do this on the practice tee. Without a golf ball in front of you, take your stance, *close your eyes* and swing. You will be pleasantly surprised at how well you can "see" in your mind's eye exactly what you're doing. Corrections come easily, and when you actually swing at a ball—with your eyes open —you'll notice quick improvement.

—James R. Carpenter

Practice putting to smaller target

Here is a putting drill that will prepare you both physically and psychologically for your next round: Find a level spot with no grain on the practice green. Putt one ball against another that is one foot away. Do this until the second ball caroms straight back *every time.* Then lengthen the putt to two feet, three feet and four feet. When you can make the target ball go straight back on four-footers most of the time, you're ready. Don't start putting for the cup on the practice green; go right out on the course and play. You'll be sure to sink almost all of your "makeable" putts at the 4¼-inch hole.

—*Al Wagner*

Deal a card to draw the ball

Sliced shots are often caused by failing to sufficiently rotate your left arm and hand. To achieve the correct amount of rotation try this drill. Swing an iron with your left hand only. As you pass through the hitting area feel as though you are dealing cards with your left hand, allowing your arm and hand to gradually turn to the left. Keep this feeling and watch your shots curve left instead of right. —*Joe Sodd*

231

Get on the ball to stop swaying

To avoid straightening the right leg and rolling your weight to the outside of the right foot on your backswing—common faults among higher handicappers—try this simple practice tee exercise.

Place a golf ball under the outside of your right foot, just forward of the heel. This will concentrate your weight on the inside of your right foot and leg. Hit several full shots with a 7-iron in this manner, being sure to keep your right knee flexed on the backswing.

After you acquire the feeling of keeping your knee flexed and the weight on the inside of the right foot, remove the ball and hit several more shots. You'll find you will be making a better body turn and will be in a more balanced and powerful position to begin the downswing.

—*Kenneth Glovando*

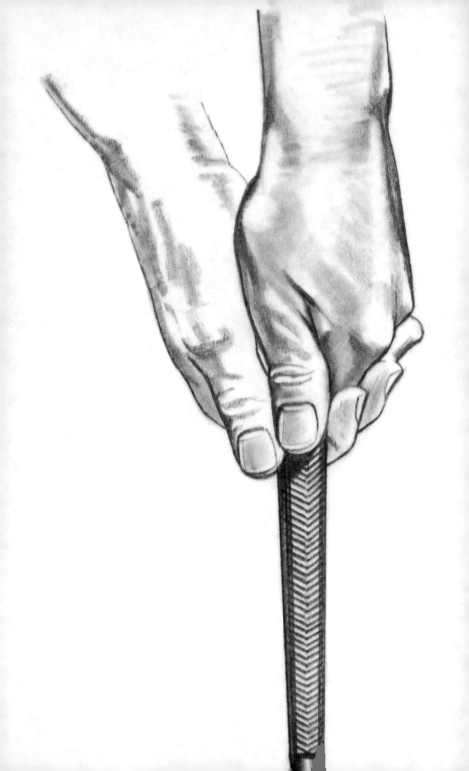

Train left-side muscles to control club

Too much "right-hand" influence is a common problem of many, if not most, golfers. To learn to control the club with your left hand, arm and side, I suggest this method of practicing.

Grip a wedge or 9-iron with only your left hand directly on the club. Place your right hand lightly over the left so all fingers overlap. Then merely practice-swing. This drill will carry over and give you left-side control when you use your regular grip during actual play. You soon will be hitting better shots than ever before.

—Stewart Sirbaugh

Shorten grip to learn long-iron feel

It is not necessary to swing the long irons any harder than you do the shorter clubs. The longer shaft and reduced clubface loft of the 2- and 3-irons will produce sufficient distance if you swing these clubs with the same feel and confidence as you do a 9-iron, for instance.

To learn this feel, "choke down" at least two inches and practice with these long irons. The shortened grip will automatically reduce your backswing and give you more control, but less distance. Once you're hitting the long irons crisply in this manner, move your hands back up to their normal position. You will retain the "short-iron" feel, but regain normal long-iron distance. —*Dave Carolan*

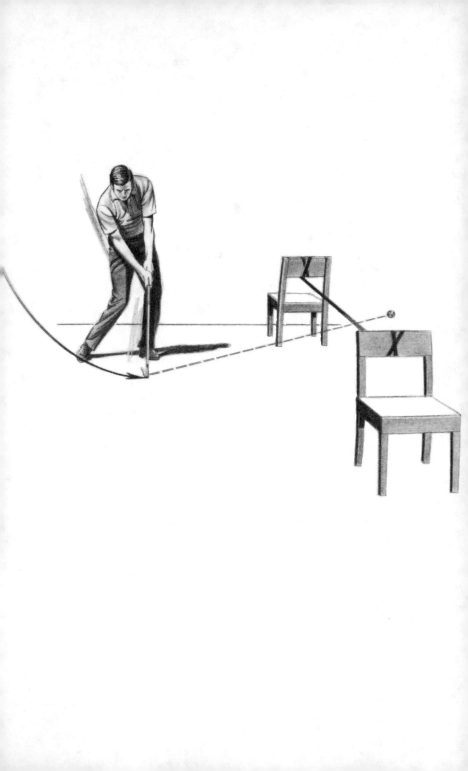

Extend fully through impact

Many golfers find it difficult to extend their arms, hands and clubhead through the ball. They attempt to "impact" the ball with an ineffectual flick of the hands. This living room drill will help you develop full extension.

Tie a ribbon between two chairs, about two-and-a-half feet above the carpet. Take a short iron (8 or 9) and a plastic ball (it won't break things) and set up for your shot about six feet from the ribbon. Make your normal pitch-shot swing but try to keep the ball under the ribbon. To hit the shot cleanly, but under the ribbon, you must make a full arm extension during and after impact. If you chop or flick at the ball, you will top it or flip it over the ribbon.   —*Irv Lightstone*

239

Thaw first-tee freeze with pre-round warm-up

Nervousness on the first tee comes from a lack of confidence; you are never sure where that first drive will go. By warming up before playing, you should be able to reduce this anxiety.

Loosen your muscles and joints gradually. Start by hitting a few pitches with a wedge or 9-iron. Then work your way down—as time permits—through the middle irons to the long irons, fairway woods and driver. After this, you should be ready to step up to the first tee relatively relaxed and confident.

—*King Carter*

241

Release right-hand grip to feel proper weight shift

The most common fault of golfers I teach is their inability to transfer their weight onto their left side early in the downswing.

The best cure I've found is to have these players actually let go of the club with the right hand at impact and then extend the left arm fully. The momentum of the clubhead pulls their weight to the left and lifts the right heel off the ground. Try this practice technique and you will experience the feeling of making a proper weight shift.

—*Fran Cipro*

Look yourself in the eye for a better address posture

An important aid to better balance at the address position is holding your head high. This will help you keep your back straight and your weight positioned equally between the balls and heels of your feet. It also will put you in good position to make a smooth swing without a droopy chin interfering with your shoulder turn.

There's an easy way to check your head position. Assume your address position with your club at the base of a full-length mirror. Look in the mirror without moving your head. If you can see no part of your body above your waist, your head droops too much. Lift your head until, by rolling your eyes upward, you can look yourself in the eye. Now you'll be in proper position.

—*Jerry Cozby*

Make your pitching a piece of cake

Place a shallow baking pan on the seat of a cushioned chair and practice pitching plastic balls into the pan on the fly. A 15-minute daily session this winter will do wonders for your short game next spring. For more fun get the whole family to compete . . . make the loser bake a cake in the pan!

—*Leo Beckmann*

Swing leaded 'club' to strengthen left side

Right-handed golfers who have relatively weak left sides often allow the right side to take over the downswing (in the case of left-handers, the left side takes over). Such overpowering of the left side leads to all kinds of swing faults.

Here's an exercise to quickly strengthen and train the left side (right side for lefties). Buy some lead wire or tape at the hardware store and wrap a couple of pounds of it around the hosel of an old sand wedge to make yourself a heavy exercise club. Choking down on the grip, swing this exercise club to the top with both hands, then swing down, through and into a high finish *with the leading hand only.*

Besides strengthening your control side, a few swings daily like this promote great extension through and beyond impact. —*Dick McGuire*

Sand wedge heft will strengthen left

To strengthen your left side this winter, practice swinging a sand wedge while holding it only with your left hand. Keep your wrist firm and make it a point to achieve good extension on either side of the ball. Using a plastic ball inside your garage or basement or a real ball outside on mild days, practice about 10 minutes daily. At first it will be difficult to make solid contact, but as your left hand, arm and side become stronger, you will find it easier. Next spring your left side will be conditioned to play its proper leading role in the swing. —*Steve Blatnak*

Toss ball gently to learn right-hand release

The golf swing should be thought of as a right-handed, underhanded toss of the ball with a "lively" hand action. This action can easily be practiced indoors.

Set a box or other target at knee-height and station yourself 10 feet away. Hold a golf ball lightly in the fingers of your right hand, take a normal golf stance and toss the ball down and into the target with an underhanded motion.

Daily practice will soon ingrain the feeling of the "underhanded" aspect of the swing and a proper right-hand "release." But be sure that you always hold the ball very gently.

—Harold McGrail

As ye waggle, so shall ye swing

The waggle is a miniature swing, and if it is done correctly the full swing has a better chance of following suit. For this reason the waggle should be done only behind the ball in the approximate path of the full swing. Players who waggle the clubhead over the ball introduce an unnecessary variation and are not correctly previewing the swing. As you waggle the clubhead straight back away from the target, special attention should be paid to the left wrist. It should be hinged (or cocked) so that the back of the left hand is kept in a flat relationship with the arm at the top of the backswing.

With daily practice over the winter months, you can have the waggle incorporated into your swing by the time the season opens.   —*Tommy Smith*